D1120710

Cover: The Kulhan family in Rome on April 30, 2000, during the
canonization ceremony of Sister Maria Faustina Kowalska, with the Slovak
Ambassador to the Vatican, Marian Servatka and his wife Viera.

ISBN: 1-4196-9905-9
ISBN-13: 9781419699054

Visit www.booksurge.com to order additional copies.

TRIUMPH Through TRIAL

The Untold Story Behind the Canonization of
Sister Maria Faustina Kowalska

By
Joseph P. Kenney

Acknowledgements

I am deeply indebted to my loving wife, Sonia, who is my constant source of support and inspiration. I am also most grateful to the Kulhan family for allowing me the honor of publishing their incredible story. I also wish to thank Father Seraphim Michalenko and Father Larry Gesy for their spiritual guidance and support throughout this project. Above all, I am indebted to the extraordinary grace of Divine Mercy.

Dedicated to the Hidden Flower
"Jesus loves hidden souls. A hidden flower is the most fragrant"
(Diary of Saint Faustina, paragraph 275)

Contents

Foreword

*The Singular Slovak-American Contribution
Toward the Canonization of a Polish Saint*
by Father Stanislaus Seraphim Michalenko, MIC

Vice Postulator for North America in the Canonization Cause
of Sr. Maria Faustina Kowalska of the Congregation of Sisters
of Our Lady of Mercy, Director of the John Paul II Institute of
Divine Mercy, Stockbridge, Massachusetts, U.S.A.

Never did it cross the minds of the Kulhans, a family in the United States of America from Slovak roots, that they, an in particular the mother, Marta, and the podiatrist daughter, Dr. Darline, would be crucially instrumental in the verification of the miracle that made possible, on Divine Mercy Sunday of the Great Jubilee Year 2000, the timely addition to the glorious list of Canonized Saints the first native-born Polish woman in the 2000-year history of the Church, and the more than 1000 year history of Christian Poland.

It could likewise never have been foreseen that Fr. Stanislaus Seraphim Michalenko, an American Greek-Catholic priest of paternal Slovak roots, and member of the Congregation of Marians of the Immaculate Conception of the Most Blessed Virgin Mary-the first Religious Order of men founded in Poland by a Pole, should also have played a key role in the Canonization Process of Saint Maria Faustina Kowalska as her Cause's Vice-Postulator for North America. He was a witness to the first miracle attributed to Saint Faustina's intercession that opened the way for her Beatification in 1993, as well as the coordinator of the efforts that served to verify that miracle and a second one which made possible the adding of the Religious Sister to the list of Catholic Saints on April 30, 2000.

The Kulhans and Fr. Michalenko met at the National Shrine of The Divine Mercy, of which the latter was then Rector, in Stockbridge, Massachusetts, U.S.A. The occasion was Marta Kulhan's 70th Birthday and the visit to the Shrine was the special Birthday gift she requested of her family.

That meeting was the setting of a conversation concerning the second miracle that was being attributed to the Polish nun's intercession. On hearing some details about the reported healing, Dr. Darline recognized a situation, akin to her own experience with a medication she no longer needed, that ultimately provided a key clue to the establishing the fact, that the Reverend Ron Pytel's heart was miraculously restored to normal on the night of October 5, 1995. Following a service of prayer for his healing and blessing with a relic of then Blessed Faustina Kowalska, the priest took a prescribed dose of medication that he had forgotten to take earlier, and soon begun to sense physical distress with every deep breath, something that he had not experienced using the medication up that time.

Attributing the effect he experienced to having over-exerted himself that day, it was only after plunging himself into the taxing duties of parish activity during the next few days-which happened to be full of feverish preparations for the Holy Father's visit to the city of Baltimore, Maryland, and his parish's participation in it- that the priest realized he was operating with physical strength that up to that time he was deprived of by a heart ailment, from which he was suffering since birth, but of which he had been unaware until it was discovered during a medical visit intended to deal with allergies. After the October 5th healing service he was feeling physical distress only shortly after taking his daily dose of medication that was supposed to help improve the functioning of his heart with its new artificial valve and drastically enlarged left ventricle.

Dr. Darline immediately applied herself to a search for information on the possible side effects of the medication Fr. Pytel was taking. It led her from one expert in the field to another higher one, until she was directed to arguably the most competent cardiologist in the country, the first individual to earn cardiology's "triple crown" from the world's three major cardiologic organizations, Dr. Valentin Fuster, M.D. Ph.D., of The Mount Sinai Medical Center in New York City, at the time the President of the American Heart Association.

When on a visit to his own eminent cardiologist (Dr. Nicholas Fortuin, of the renowned Johns Hopkins Hospital in Baltimore, Maryland, who was the first to discover a dramatic change in the condition of his patient's heart) Fr. Ron Pytel mentioned that he had been to see Dr. Fuster, who agreed to carefully examine his case, the surprised Dr. Fortuin-knowing, evidently, how difficult it was to reach the very famous and very busy cardiologist-asked, "How did you get your **foot** into his door?" Only somewhat later did Reverend Pytel realize that he could have jokingly, but truthfully, answered, "Why, thanks to a Slovak-American **podiatrist**!"

There can be **no doubt whatever**, that it was the **devoted, long** and **unrelenting** effort on the part of Dr. Darline Kulhan, to verify and establish the facts that would clearly show the healing of the Rev. Pytel's heart as having been immediate, complete, and lasting, and unable to be explained naturally or scientifically, that enabled the miraculous nature of the healing to be acknowledged by the Catholic Church as attributed to the Polish "Blessed" just in time for The Great Jubilee Year 2000, on the threshold of the Third Millennium of Christianity, as, in the words of Pope John Paul II, "God's gift to our time."

However, Dr. Darline would not have been able to bring the work to conclusion on time if she were not helped by practically all members of her family, who with her were relentlessly and most intensely involved in the process of searching out, identifying and correlating for Dr. Fuster the necessary data from all of the available sources in a clear and concise way, expending an incredible amount of their time and energy and even personal, financial resources.

Of particular importance to this effort were her mother Marta's inspirations with literally opportune, heavenly encouragement when it was especially needed to press on with the work in the face of many (and oftentimes painful) obstacles, that kept springing up from all sorts of sources (even from some that one would not have expected), seemingly designed to impede progress toward the goal. Not in the least to be overlooked, too, was the invaluable editorial assistance of her sister, Sonia, and the generous service rendered by her young son Harry, with his computer expertise.

Only the actual witnesses to the Kulhan family's combined and persistent efforts are able adequately to appraise the greatness of its crucial contribution to the very possibility of St. Marie Faustina's canonization taking place during the Great Jubilee Year, and particularly on the First Sunday after Easter-the day Jesus insisted with her, that she must do everything in her power to have it solemnly celebrated in the Church as the Feast of Mercy.

The facts: 1) of the solemn addition of Sr. Faustina to the list of Saints (an infallible action of the Church), and 2) of the Holy Father's declaration in his homily on that occasion, that henceforth in the whole Church the Second Sunday of Easter will be called Divine Mercy Sunday (in explicit fulfillment of Our Lord's desire for the establishment of the Feast of Mercy, revealed to the Church through this humble Religious Sister), serve as the validation of the truth of her revelations from the Lord concerning the Divine Mercy Message and its allied Devotion, which she was instrumental in making known to the whole world through her spiritual Diary. The Holy Father himself quoted these revelations, declaring in his canonization homily:

Jesus told Sr. Faustina: "**Humanity will not find peace until it turns trustfully to divine mercy**" (Diary, manuscript, Notebook 1, page 130),

and he continued:

Through the work of this Polish religious, this message has become linked forever to the 20th century, the last of the second millennium and the bridge to the third. It is not a new message but can be considered a gift of special enlightenment that helps us to relive the Gospel of Easter more intensely, to offer it as a ray of light to the men and women of our time.

What will the years ahead bring us? What will man's future on earth be like? We are not given to know. However, it is certain that in addition to new progress there will unfortunately be no lack of painful experiences. But the light of divine mercy, which the Lord in a way wished to return to the world through Sr. Faustina's charism, will illuminate the way for men and women into the third millennium.

Further on the Holy Father stated:

Sr. Faustina's canonization has a particular eloquence: **by this act I intend today to pass this message on to the new millennium. I pass it on to all people,** so that they will learn to know ever better the true face of God and the true face of their brethren.

Thanks to the validation that the act of her canonization gives to the revelations granted to St. M. Faustina, and thanks to the Holy Father's statements regarding the importance that the message of these revelations holds for the Church and for the world, two things claim our particular attention. First of all, we are witnesses to the fulfillment of a prophecy recorded in St. Faustina's Diary, namely:

There will come a time when this work, which God is demanding so very much, will be as though utterly undone. And then God will act with great power, which will give evidence of its authenticity. It will be **a new splendor** for the Church, although **it has been dormant in it from long ago** (manuscript Notebook 1, p. 160).

The spreading of Sr. Faustina's revelations and of the devotions inspired by them was forbidden by the Church for 20 years!

Secondly, it can be expected that St. Maria Faustina's greatest mission is only now about to unfold. That mission was impressed upon her both by the Blessed Mother and her divine Son who told her:

You will prepare the world for My final coming.
(Diary, manuscript Notebook 1, page 170);
and
I gave the Savior to the world; as for you, you have to speak to the world about His great mercy and prepare the world for the Second Coming of Him who will come, not as a merciful Savior, but as a just Judge.
(Diary, manuscript Notebook II, pages 90, 91.)

The pivotal contribution of Slovak-Americans toward the coming about of what has been related above, therefore, is not an insignificant matter. The Divine Mercy Message and Devotion, of whose spreading throughout the world St. Faustina was God's elect instrument, cannot be regarded as a "Polish invention or Polish reserve" promoted by a Polish Pope. In light of Our Lord's revelations to her **they are heaven's sheet anchor [a person or thing to be relied upon in danger or emergency (*Webster's New World Dictionary*)]** for a drowning humanity (Diary, manuscript Notebook II, pages 305 and 319). Either we take hold of it or we perish, for Jesus gave Sr. Faustina this command:

> Write: Before I come as a just Judge, I first open wide the door of My mercy. He who refuses to pass through the door of My mercy must pass through the door of My justice! (Diary, manuscript Notebook III, page 39).

It is only fitting at this point to join our Holy Father, Pope John Paul II, in the prayer with which he concluded his canonization homily:

> And you, Faustina, a gift of God to our time, a gift from the land of Poland to the whole Church, obtain for us an awareness of the depths of divine mercy; help us to have a living experience of it and to bear witness to it among our brothers and sisters. May your message of light and hope spread throughout the world, spurring sinners to conversion, calming rivalries and hatred and opening individuals and nations to the practice of brotherhood. Today, fixing our gaze with you on the face of the risen Christ, let us make our own your prayer of trusting abandonment and say with firm hope: Christ Jesus, I trust in You! Jezu ufam tobie!(L'OSSERVATORE ROMANO, Weekly Edition in English 3 May 2000)

Introduction

"When I took the Messenger of the Sacred Heart into my hand and read the account of the canonization of Saint Andrew Bobola, my soul was instantly filled with a great longing that our Congregation too might have a saint, and I wept like a child that there was no saint in our Midst. And the Lord Jesus said to me, **Don't cry. You are that saint**. Then the light of God inundated my soul, and I was given to know how much I was to suffer, and I said to the Lord, How will that come about? And the Lord answered: **It is not for you to know how this will come about**." (Diary of Saint Faustina, paragraph 1650).

Almost all Catholics know of Saint Faustina and the devotion of Divine Mercy she promulgated. However, very few know the incredible story of the Kulhan family and their substantial role in the fulfillment of this prophecy. It is the story of the American Dream in its grandest sense. It is the story of faith and inspiration for all who struggle to follow God's laws and to do His will, no matter what the sacrifice.

I have tried earnestly to get their story published, without success. Therefore, I have taken the initiative to self-publish a book of my own. Though discouraged, I have been able to take solace in the struggle of the Kulhan family and in Our Lord's words to Saint Faustina: "**Do as much as is in your power, and don't worry about the rest. These difficulties prove that this work is Mine. Be at peace so long as you do all that is within your power**." (Diary of Saint Faustina, paragraph 1295).

Chapter 1, The Soldier

"You gave Me great glory today by fighting so faithfully.
Let it be confirmed and engraved on your heart that I am
always with you, even if you don't feel my presence at the
time of battle." (Diary of Saint Faustina, paragraph 1499).

When I was on active duty a few years ago, I was asked during a leadership seminar which person I admired most. My response was swift and certain: John Kulhan, my father-in-law. Although my friends and relatives are impressed with what they consider is my past distinguished military career, including combat in Iraq, compared to John Kulhan I am not fit to carry his sandals. It is with him that this amazing story starts.

John Kulhan was born to John and Stephanie Kulhan, on October 1, 1922, in Dolnysiles, Slovakia. He was the second-oldest son in a family of 11 children. From an early age his father taught him the challenge and sacrifice involved in being a political activist. His father had served as an officer during the Slovak war of independence against the Austrian-Hungarian Empire and had been wounded during a battle in present-day Bosnia. Nevertheless, he was able to return to his hotel business and continue his advocacy for a greater, independent Slovakia. The area in which he lived had become a part of Hungary after World War I but the majority of the population was Slovak. The Hungarian Government, therefore, viewed his father's activism as a threat and forced him to flee to Bosany, Slovakia, in 1938, leaving behind all of the possessions he had worked so hard to earn. His older brother, Joe, tried to stop the police from taking down the Slovak flag in the town's center and was shot in the arm. John would be the next member of his family to pay for the freedom of his country.

John Kulhan on the Day he was commissioned in the Slovak Army

After high school John entered technical school, only to be drafted into the Slovak Army in 1942 at the height of World War II. He soon found himself fighting a much larger Russian Army on the Eastern Front. While trying to retreat, the German Army engaged his unit. Poorly equipped, out-gunned, and out-manned, he was captured by the Russians and became a prisoner of war. Times were very bleak then but he clung to his faith and hoped for a better day. This came with a political alliance that re-formed his unit into the Czechoslovakian Army in Exile, a force now tasked to fight with the Russians against the Germans after the Slovak uprising against Nazi occupation. As a newly appointed officer, he traveled to Vladivostok to retrieve equipment from the United States for his unit. This was the first time he would come into contact with Americans and their weaponry. He remembered being very impressed with the quality and durability of the American trucks and jeeps he procured, and was very grateful for the generosity of the American people. The next time he went into battle with his soldiers, things would be different.

The survival skills John had learned on the Russian Front served him well in this new campaign to purge the Nazis from Southern Poland in the battle for the Krasna oil fields. His assignment was to gain intelligence on enemy locations and movements. In one extraordinary act of heroism, he slipped deep into enemy territory, captured a German officer in his bunker, and turned him over to Allied forces for interrogation. With the advantage of freshly acquired intelligence and American equipment, he led his soldiers on to Dukla Pass, the bloody engagement that would be the turning point in the liberation of Slovakia.

Lieutenant John Kulhan prepares his unit for the Dukla Pass Offensive

Close to 50,000 soldiers would perish in this three-month campaign, which began on October 5, 1944, the future feast day of Saint Faustina and the sixth anniversary of her death. John Kulhan later described it as so horrible that pieces of human remains rained down on him from the trees, literally soaking him in blood. He would play a critical role, moving his artillery battery up a mountain pass by night to launch a surprise attack upon now known German positions. The actions of his unit proved critical in the subsequent breakthrough of tanks and infantry that would eventually put the Germans to route. Slovakia was free, or so it seemed.

The Russians took credit for liberating Slovakia but it was the Slovak Army in Exile that bore the brunt of the offensive and suffered the heaviest casualties. Afterwards, General Ludvik Svboda awarded John Kulhan the coveted Order of the White Eagle for gallantry in action. Today, at Dukla Pass, a museum stands in honor of the thousands who perished in this horrific battle.

Throughout the remainder of the war, Lieutenant Kulhan would continue to launch raids against the Germans from his base in the Tatra Mountains. After three years of bloody engagements he was wounded, just two weeks before the end of World War II. This was the start of a pattern of fortune and misfortune that unraveled in the years ahead. Throughout it all, he would bounce back, stronger than ever before.

While recovering in a military hospital, John Kulhan started to think about the nice girl who had waved good-bye to him as he had left for war with so much uncertainty about its outcome. She was a good friend of his sister Geta and both had worked in the local hospital for several years, caring for wounded soldiers near her home in Bosany. Thoughts of her eased his pain and it was there, amongst his dying and wounded brothers in arms, that he resolved to find this young lady and marry her. Her name was Marta Baluch.

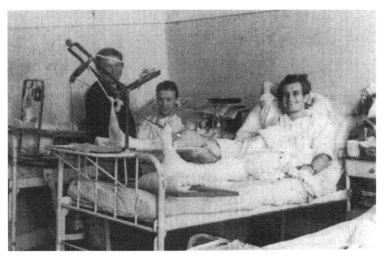

John Kulhan, wounded but optimistic, recovers at a military hospital

Two years later she would say "yes" to him as Marta Kulhan. Their marriage would be a blessing to each other, one that would grow even stronger with the extreme sacrifices to come. But on that day, September 29, 1946, John Kulhan would not feel or even think about the pain of his wounds because this was the happiest day of his life. Unfortunately, this era of happiness would end the following year.

John and Marta Kulhan on their wedding day at Saint Martin
Catholic Church, Bosany, Slovakia, September 29, 1946

Chapter 2, The Dissident

*"How frightful is this exile! How terrible this wilderness
I have to cross!"* (Diary of Saint Faustina,
paragraph 1606).

In the worldly sense, things were really looking good for
the new family as John and Marta reached their first high point.
John had started a thriving retail business and had accumulated
land and livestock to further augment his wealth. Because of his
distinguished military service, he was offered the opportunity
to attend the most renowned military academy in Russia,
guaranteeing him an eventual promotion to General. He turned
down this offer but did accept an appointment as advisor to his
nation's newly formed provisional parliament. As a leader in
his country's democratic movement, he found himself in direct
conflict with the Communists, who occupied and controlled
his county. He could easily have kept his wealth and influential
position if only he had supported these atheistic forces instead
of attacking them. But he refused to join the Communists for
the same reasons he had turned down a promising military
career. Simply put, Communism was contrary to his religion
and a free society, and he would not compromise on his stance.
On the contrary, he directly challenged the newly appointed
Communist prime minister and all his cronies. The consequences
would be swift and severe.

While John was away on a business trip, one of his friends
contacted him and warned him not to return to his hometown.
The Communists had seized his business and had frozen all
of his assets. They had also decided to arrest him and execute
him as an American spy. John was shocked. The country for
which he had spent three years fighting for during World War
II had not only just abandoned him but had turned on him.

His wounds and decorations were of no value to this puppet government now. However, he did return home to say good-bye to his lovely wife and daughter, Ann Marie. With only $20.00 in his pocket, he gave $10.00 to Marta, kept $10.00 for himself, and left his country. During this good-bye he also learned that Marta was pregnant again, which made his departure even more difficult and emotional. He promised Marta he would return, and she never doubted him. This would become another low point for John and Marta but they knew their faith in God would get them through it, in ways that would prove to be miraculous.

John had little difficulty escaping from his native country. He knew the land, and his survival skills were well honed after struggling through three years of relentless combat. While traveling out of the country on a train, his keen intuition told him to strike up a conversation with two young men who, in his words, "didn't quite seem to fit in." He was not surprised to later learn that they were American intelligence agents. One of these agents later became a good friend of his, but to this day, he does not know the agent's real name. In response to what the Communists had done to him and his family, John shared his extensive knowledge of the military and political environment of his native land with the American intelligence service. One reason he did it was to stop what he considered an atheistic threat to a way of life personified by what could best be described as "The American Dream." John Kulhan's faith and freedom were being besieged by this satanic philosophy, and he was determined to challenge this force in whatever way he could. He was not content just to provide information about what he knew. No, he would do much more.

John had attributed his survival on the battlefield and during his escape not to his physical strength but to his intuition. He believed he could literally "smell a Communist." Whatever the talent it was he had, it was not questioned by the intelligence community. On several occasions he identified Communist agents and then assisted with their apprehension. On one top secret mission he followed two spies on a cloak and dagger mission through several countries up to their arrest less than a block away from the safety of their consulate. During this year and a half of separation from his family, he refined his surveillance and evasion skills to perfection. They would soon prove their worth.

John escaped the wrath of the Communists but his family did not. Marta bore the brunt of their attacks. The police would show up unannounced and storm into her house at all hours of the night looking for her husband. They threatened her and smashed the family's furniture in their attempts to break her. She pleaded with them to leave her and her two young daughters in peace, insisting that her husband had left and was not in Slovakia. The Communists even took away her ration card, leaving her totally dependent upon her family to share their limited allocation of food. Many of her friends told her to forget about her husband ever returning and encouraged her to remarry. Marta wouldn't think of it, and she made that quite clear to those who would even suggest it (they would do so only once). The Communists, however, were still intent on destroying the Kulhan family.

John's escape right under their noses had become a source of embarrassment, and it had encouraged others to escape and speak out about the oppressive rule of their nation's dictatorship. Officials ordered Marta to denounce her husband on the radio and to say he had abandoned his family. Marta refused, so the Communists decided to attack her through her children. They gave her this ultimatum:Either you do what we say or you will go to prison and we will send your two children to a Communist re-education camp. All she could do was "Trust in God" to rescue her from what appeared to be an impossible situation. John's sister, Geta, knowing the strain Marta was under, invited her over for a visit. She had remained a good friend of Marta ever since she had introduced her to John. Besides, she sensed that Marta needed to get away from the harassment of the Communists, even if it was only for a few days. When Marta arrived at Geta's house and opened the door, there stood her husband, John Kulhan.

She couldn't believe it!!! He had slipped back into Slovakia to rescue his family. He had made good on his promise to return one day. His friends in the American intelligence community had told him, "Don't do this; it's suicide!" But John would hear none of it. He knew he had the skills to succeed but that he would need more help. So he offered prayers for nine days to Our Lady of Perpetual Help and, trusting in her protection, embarked upon what would become a most incredible journey.

He took a job as a farm laborer on the Austrian border, working without pay to study the terrain and movements of the border guards. Then he snuck across the fence undetected. Three days later he entered Bratislava through an extraordinary act courage and ingenuity. The bridge over the Danube River into the city had an unexpected checkpoint. To make it through, he quickly grabbed the arm of a lady who passed by the checkpoint every day. Believing him to be a Communist agent, she went along with his deception. The guards, thinking he was a friend of hers, let him walk past without checking his identification. Little did they know that this gentleman passing by was one their most wanted political dissidents.

John told Marta they would leave the next day for Austria and then on to the United States, as he had just secured political refugee status. Marta never questioned his decision, nor did she worry about what lay ahead. Her trust in God was her source of hope and consolation. She also believed wholeheartedly in her husband and his ability to lead them to safety. They left in a taxi the next day and took it as far as they could. Then, by cover of night, they crossed the border under the wire, on their hands and knees, Marta carrying Ann Marie and John carrying their nine-month-old daughter, Jean. John had timed the guards' patrols and had detected the most vulnerable point in their fence. But as they were going through, Jean got caught in the wire and started to cry.

As they remained motionless, they could hear one of the guards saying that a child from the nearby town must be crying up a storm. The guards then walked away. After all, nobody would expect a baby to be crying at a border fence at night, right? The family made it through and continued their escape up a nearby hill. Only when they reached the crest of the hill did the guards notice them. Realizing they had let a family escape, they started to shoot in their direction. The couple ran as fast as they could and jumped over the ridge, with bullets falling just short of their mark. The worst was over, but they were not yet safe.

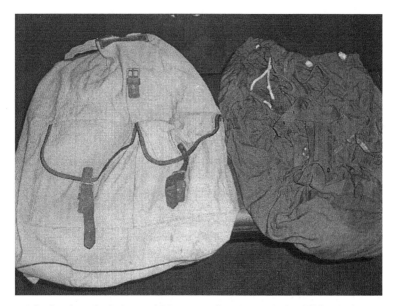

The backpacks John and Marta used to carry their children, Ann Marie and Jean, across the border

At the time, Austria was still an occupied country. John had managed to get his family to Vienna without being detected but he left Marta with the children in a park while he went to the American Embassy to get visas for his family. What he had not realized was that he had left them in the Russian zone. One of the Russian soldiers didn't recognize Marta as a regular who visited the park so he walked up to her and asked for her identification. What was she to do now? How would God help her? Miraculously, a stranger sitting next to her told the soldier Marta was a friend who was visiting. The guard believed her, and left.

John realized his mistake after he departed the embassy and rushed back to get his family. He was relieved to see them in the park where he had left them. As they were leaving the Russian zone, the Communist guard did not notice Marta's false passport. He just yelled at her to keep moving. Then, as they entered the American zone, the U. S. soldier looked at Marta's passport several times. Recognizing it as false, he laughed, and waved the family through as their daughter Ann Marie asked: "Why was this soldier so nice when the last one was so mean?" The family's escape was made complete with their arrival at a refugee camp in Salzburg, Austria.

The journey to America was not without obstacles. Getting the visas was relatively easy compared to what lay ahead. John and Marta boarded a ship to cross the Atlantic Ocean with their two children, Anna Marie and Jean. Soon after leaving port their ship, the General Greeley, collided with another vessel while trying to navigate through dense fog. They waited nervously as the crew decided whether or not to abandon ship. This was especially scary for Marta who was now pregnant with their third child, Darline. After some structural repairs, the captain decided to continue with the voyage at half speed. Such was the ongoing story of the family; for them nothing came easy. Eventually, the ship arrived in New York Harbor. The

Kulhans, like so many other immigrants before them, passed by the Statue of Liberty and on to their new life. They arrived in the United States without knowing the language, without any money, and without any family or friends to support them. What they did have was their faith.

Although John's wife and children were now safe, his family in Slovakia continued to suffer. The Communists arrested John's oldest brother, Joe, and he was forced to work in the state's coal-mine prison camp. The inhumane conditions there ultimately destroyed his health and led to his early demise. John's father died in his early 60s, the year he left Slovakia. When I spoke to his brother-in-law in Slovakia recently, he told me the family had always believed the father had been poisoned. This method of elimination was not uncommon for those who threatened the Communists and their agendas. Such Barbarism has come to light only now, with the recent elections in Ukraine where Viktor Yushchenko, an advocate for freedom, was poisoned by his opponents but lived to become the nation's president.

Seeing such cruelty inflicted upon his family, John helped his two younger brothers escape from Communist Slovakia. One, Jerry, would settle with him in the United States. The other, Julius, would become a citizen of Australia.

After proceeding through New York City, the Kulhan family moved to Saginaw Bay, Michigan, where John had found a sponsor. A few months later Darline was born, and a year later, his son Johnny arrived. John's job, by worldly accounts, was quite demeaning. During the war he had led hundreds of soldiers under his command. Now he found himself supervising dozens of cows, working as a farmhand with a wife and four children to support.

Financially it was difficult, but they got by. Oftentimes John and Marta would fast so their children would have enough to eat. On one Christmas John constructed a tree for the family out of a broomstick. Throughout these tough times, the family never even considered applying for public assistance. No, the United States had been good to them and they were not about to take advantage of its generosity. As time went on, John's English improved and he gained the confidence to return to the Big Apple of New York City. Many blessings would come to John and Marta here, including the birth of their youngest child, Sonia.

John Kulhan, third from left, with his family at the outbreak of World War II with his brother Joe, second from right and sister Geta, second from left

Chapter 3, The Activist

"In difficult moments, I will fix my gaze upon the silent Heart of Jesus, stretched upon the Cross, and from the exploding flames of His merciful Heart, will flow down upon me the strength to keep fighting."

(Diary of Saint Faustina, paragraph 906).

Immediately upon his arrival in New York, John Kulhan the soldier became John Kulhan the political activist. The Communists had done everything they could to destroy him and his family. Now he would fight back, this time from a free country where he wouldn't be arrested or executed for his political views. He would become Secretary of the Slovak National Congress and a founding member of the Captive Nation Society. He would organize protests against Nikita Khrushchev when he visited the United Nations in New York City on the day he would give his infamous "we will bury you" speech. He took the initiative in these roles to lobby Congress and the Presidency on the dangers of Communism. Through his contacts, he learned that Fidel Castro was plotting to turn Cuba into a Communist Dictatorship. He sent several letters of warning to members of Congress and the President in the late 1950s detailing what he knew. Years later the White House thanked him and confirmed that what he had said had been true. Unfortunately, it was too late as all that he had predicted had come to pass.

John Kulhan, to the right of the center sign, at a political rally protesting against Nikita Khrushchev's visit to the United Nations (daughter Darline is in front of him and son Johnny is under the center sign)

John Kulhan, second from left, meets with Vice President Richard Nixon as a Slovak delegate of the Captive Nation Society

However, the most challenging and dangerous confrontation with the evil forces of Communism came in 1968 when Russia invaded Czechoslovakia. John just happened to be in the country, visiting President Ludvik Svoboda, the former general under whom he had served during World War II. The two of them had maintained a solid bond, one that only fellow soldiers could understand, as they had saved each other's lives on the Russian Front. John was with Ludvik when the news arrived of the Russian invasion. Ludvik told John: "We are no longer free," then told him to leave while he still could. It was the last time these two warriors would see each other.

John managed to escape from Prague on the back of his friend's motorcycle during the height of the invasion. He then took a train to rescue his wife and daughter Sonia in Bosany. On the way, two gentlemen approached him and asked him to help condemn the Russian invasion of Czechoslovakia. He agreed and, once again, he would risk his life opposing Communist oppression. This time he was assigned the task of bringing hundreds of thousands of signatures of Slovak citizens to the United Nations protesting the Russian invasion. John Kulhan never found out who these two men were. But that didn't matter to John Kulhan. He was a man on a mission.

Upon his arrival in Bosany, Marta rushed to greet John and shouted: "The Communists were already here looking for you!" So they packed and left within one minute. To ensure the safety of his family, John left separately in his rental car, with the signatures he had accumulated hidden in the spare tire. His vehicle was searched several times before he crossed the Austrian border but Providence ordained that none of the guards would search the spare tire. They searched everywhere else in the car, including inside the seats, which they tore open with their bayonets. If they had found these petitions, John Kulhan would undoubtedly have been executed. Upon his return home to New York City, he personally took these petitions to his contacts at the United Nations Security Council and several countries, relying in part on these petitions, condemned the Russian invasion of Czechoslovakia. The Communists were baffled as to how these documents made it to this international forum. Only now do they have their answer. John would continue to wage his crusade against the Communists for the next 35 years.

His efforts reached a climax on March 29, 2003 on the White House lawn in Washington, DC, when Slovakia joined NATO. I had the privilege of being there with him on this famous day. He insisted on arriving four hours early to have a front-row view of President George W. Bush and Slovak Prime Minister Mikulas Dzurinda together.

John Kulhan and author on the White House Lawn after Slovakia
NATO Induction Ceremony

The wait was physically draining for me but not for John Kulhan who, at the age of 81, stood there with me the whole time, never wavering, despite his war wounds, which cause him discomfort to this day. He witnessed firsthand his nation entering into an alliance with the United States. He had finally won his battle against the Communists.

This conflict would finally be laid to rest two years later, on October 5, 2005, in Svidnik, Slovakia, when John returned to commemorate the Battle of Dukla Pass 61 years after he had fought there with his fellow veterans. On that day, former Communists and freedom fighters united as one in a free country embraced each other and exchanged stories of survival and heroism.

I was once again honored to witness this event firsthand. As with the ceremony on the White House lawn, John did not waiver. Now, at the age of 83, he stood and marched in processions for several hours at five locations over two days. He received the Dukla Pass Medal of Freedom at a public ceremony in the City Hall, attended by local authorities and media. However, his greatest honor was when his fellow veterans chose him to lay a wreath at the statue of General Ludvik Svoboda, whom he had so admired. Everywhere he went, he told his story and that of the Slovak Army in Exile, especially to the youth who had no idea of its existence, thanks to years of Communist propaganda.

John Kulhan, far right, marches with his fellow veterans at the
Dukla Pass Memorial Ceremony, Svdnik, Slovakia, October 6, 2005

John Kulhan stays in continual contact with the curator
of the National Museum to this day, making sure future
generations will never forget. He also has the distinction of
being the last known surviving Slovak-American veteran of
this bloody campaign. I remember him talking to the museum
manager, Dr. John Rodak, at the close of our visit to Svidnik
about how he had saved General Ludvik Svoboda by shoving
him out of a bunker seconds before an artillery shell landed
on their position. With amazement, Dr. Rodak informed us
that General Svoboda had mentioned in his memoirs how a
young officer had saved his life during World War II exactly
has he had just described it, but that his identity had remained
a mystery (until now).

John Kulhan finally receives the Dukla Pass Medal of Freedom on October 6, 2005, in Svidnik, Slovakia, 61 years after he had fought to liberate Slovakia

John Kulhan after laying a wreath at the General Svoboda Memorial
in Svidnik, Slovakia, October 6, 2005

Chapter 4, The Inspiration

"It is not for the success of a work, but for the suffering that I give reward. "
(Diary of Saint Sister M. Faustina, paragraph 89).

Between the Kulhan family's return to New York City and their closure with the Communists the struggle had continued. Marta would climb five flights of stairs several times a day with her four children to their two bedroom apartment in Manhattan while John worked two, sometimes three, jobs to support them. Eventually, he got a break and obtained a well-paying job in the printing industry as the operations manager of a major publisher. He would put all his children through college. Two would earn Master's degrees from Fordham University, one would graduate from Medical School, and another would attend the Vienna Austria Conservatory of music.

John's daughter Jean, an accomplished ballerina, went on to win the beauty pageant for Ms Rockland County, New York. She then entered the beauty pageant for Ms. New York where she won the audience over with her talent. She seemed destined to attend the Miss America Beauty Pageant in Atlantic City. The family had made it to the second high point of their life. Where else could an immigrant family like them come to a new country with so little and accomplish so much? Unfortunately, once again, the time for rejoicing was short. In fact, it ended that night.

Jean Kulhan rehearses before the 1969 Miss New York Beauty Pageant

Although Jean had convinced the audience that she deserved to be Miss New York, the judges decided otherwise, and gave her the first runner-up title instead. Why this occurred remains a mystery but it marked the beginning of the next tragic phase of pain and suffering for the Kulhans. This time it would be the children who would bear the brunt of it. How the family managed to persevere through it was a miracle in and of itself. Yet their suffering would not be in vain. As those of faith know, it is in the darkest times that God's light shines the brightest. The Bible is full of such inspirational stories: Job, Joseph of Canaan, and Moses are just a few. And so, too, would the Kulhan family rise, as they had before, out of the ashes of despair to an even greater glory, one that would resonate worldwide.

The turning point would come 26 years later, through the matriarch of the family, Marta Kulhan. If John was the family's towering structure, Marta was the foundation upon which it stood. John Kulhan readily admits that had it not been for the steadfast love and support of his lovely wife Marta he never would have had the courage to sneak back into Slovakia and rescue his family, nor would he have been able to endure the hardships that followed.

She was always there for him, through thick and thin, for over 60 years. John Kulhan would meet many Slovak political dissidents throughout his life but there was one key difference between him and the others: He was one of the few who had remained true to his marriage vows and had not remarried with a wife and even children back home in their native country. Marta, his hidden source of strength, would now be the catalyst that would propel the family to its third and everlasting high point. But this time, the Kulhan family would have the honor of sharing the fruits of their labor with Catholics throughout the world, both in this generation and in all to come.

Young Marta with her mother on the day of her first communion in
Bosnay, Slovakia, 1934

John and Marta Kulhan renew their marriage vows in commemoration of their 60th wedding anniversary at Saint Martin Catholic Church in Bosany, Slovakia on October 11, 2006

Chapter 5, The Canonization

By Dr. Darline Kulhan

"Dear Sweet Therese, tell me, shall I go to heaven?" And she answered, "Yes, you will go to heaven, Sister." "And will I be a Saint?" To which she replied, "Yes, you will be a Saint."

(Diary of Saint Faustina, paragraph 150)

God's hand continued to weave signs and wonders for the Kulhan family. His plan for the sainthood of Blessed Faustina slowly unfolded. For my mother and family it all began on June 10, 1995, in a small chapel at St. Birgitta Convent in Darien, Connecticut, where we had gathered to pray. Suddenly, her hands began to shake and she felt a strong inspiration to do penance and sacrifices for her family. Over the next few weeks she did just that, and then, on July 17, 1995, her birthday, she felt a strong calling to visit the National Shrine of The Divine Mercy at Stockbridge, Massachusetts. Wishing to make this birthday special for her, my father; my three sisters, Ann Marie, Jean, and Sonia; and my two children, Harry and Annette; and I accompanied her there.

On this first visit we met Fr. Seraphim Michalenko, Director of the Shrine and Vice Postulator for the Canonization Cause of Sr. Faustina. It is interesting to note that Fr. Michalenko's father was also a Slovak from Vranov. Marta felt a great urgency to speak with Fr. Michalenko and ask him about her inspiration. Father Michalenko told her to pray and meditate about this after praying the Chaplet of Divine Mercy at 3 p.m. every day. So, every day, she followed his counsel. Four weeks later she felt inspired to spread Divine Mercy in her homeland of Slovakia. Trusting that Divine Mercy would show her what to do, she gathered her family and set out for Slovakia with Fr. Michalenko's blessing. Thus began our family's mission to act as "Apostles of Divine Mercy."

We received our mission while visiting a chapel in Praznovce, Slovakia, an affiliate parish of Marta's neighboring hometown, Bosany. Fifty years ago a church was to have been built next to the chapel. Supplies were ordered but before any work could begin, the Communist Government confiscated all materials and the church was forgotten. Over the years the local people yearned for the church's completion and had slowly begun collecting money.

When my mother approached the 119-year-old chapel, she felt a burning desire to support the building of this church and consecrate it to Divine Mercy. At this point our entire family knew it had received its first major project in spreading Divine Mercy. Working through St. John Nepomucene Church in New York City, we managed to collect the required funds and watch the dream of this church become a reality. In April 1997, Bishop Rabek of Nitra, Slovakia, consecrated the church ground and construction began, 50 years off schedule. However, God had more in store for our family.

While the church was being built, we continued to visit the National Shrine of The Divine Mercy. On one of these visits, Fr. Michalenko presented our family with a first-class relic of Sr. Faustina. Praying with it in her house, Marta felt an even greater closeness to this nun and gained a much greater interest in her cause for canonization. She prayed that God would lead the family accordingly. This would come a year after the church's consecration.

Holy Rosary Church in Praznovce, Slovakia, financed in part
through donations obtained by the Kulhan family

In March 1998, during one of our visits to the National
Shrine of The Divine Mercy, Fr. Seraphim, knowing I was a
doctor, asked me about the side-effects of the drug Zestril. He
said that a priest of Polish descent in Baltimore, Maryland, Fr.
Ron Pytel, whom I did not know at the time, had been prescribed
this medication after heart surgery in 1995. After taking it for
a short time, his parish prayed over him after mass, seeking the
intercession of Sr. Faustina for his healing. That night, after
taking his prescribed dose of Zestril, Fr. Pytel experienced chest
pains. When his physician, Dr. Nicholas Fortuin, examined
him, Fr. Pytel's heart was diagnosed as normal.

Fr. Michalenko wanted to know why Zestril may have caused
Fr. Pytel's chest pains. I told him I did not know the pharmacology
of the medication but that I would research it. Thus began the
final quest towards the investigation of the second miracle needed

for the canonization of then Blessed Faustina. From this day forward, whenever we would visit the National Shrine of Divine Mercy, Fr. Michalenko would receive correspondence from Rome regarding the details of this healing. At the time, we did not fully realize how divine intervention was present throughout this process but it would eventually become quite clear.

As we began the investigative process, the Holy Spirit gave us signs and inspiration. On April 7, 1998, I was researching Zestril and my mother felt an inspiration for us to focus on Fr. Pytel's symptoms. Ironically, I had just received a similar inspiration earlier that day while heading home on the train from Manhattan. This insight led me to concentrate on the history of Fr. Pytel's illness before his surgery. I discovered he had had a history of congestive heart failure long before his surgery. This was a key piece of evidence in that it became obvious Fr. Pytel's heart was so irreparably damaged by these "long-standing symptoms" that he would never have lived a normal life, even after surgery.

John and Marta Kulhan with the Priests of Divine Mercy, Father Larry Gesy, left, Father Seraphim Michalenko, center, and Father Ron Pytel, Right

In investigating this crucial piece of evidence, the intra-operative echocardiogram, the Holy Spirit was at work once again, and this time He began to help us with clues to locate incomplete or missing information that would prove vital in finalizing the process. This time the inspiration would come through my sister Sonia, who was working for the Archdiocese of Hartford Office of Radio and Television. While operating a camera for daily Mass, and wearing head-phones, Sonia heard the director say, "Echo, Echo, does anyone hear an echo, as in echocardiogram?" Sonia responded immediately to this word of knowledge by alerting me to find a missing echo, needed to evaluate the severity of Fr. Pytel's symptoms. Following this lead, I located the intra-operative echocardiogram, which became the pivotal point of the entire case. This most crucial piece of evidence further substantiated the severity of Fr. Pytel's symptoms and the extensive damage to his heart. However, the process was far from complete and future trials would certainly test us.

When one accepts God's calling, the way is not always easy, but through prayer and the encouragement of those He sends to help us, God lightens the burden. There were so many details to study in this case and so many leads to follow that I found myself discouraged on many occasions. Every time, my mother was there to encourage me to keep going. I remember one time she told me, quite emphatically: "You started it, you finish it!"

Although I now knew I had the evidence I needed to substantiate this second miracle of Sr. Faustina, I did not have the ability to advocate the cause as I was not a heart surgeon. I did not know where to turn as I headed out to attend a medical conference in Washington, DC, in April of 1998. I called my sister Sonia and told her that I thought I was at a dead end with this cause. In frustration, she shouted out to me, "You are in Washington, so do something!" Just then the Holy Spirit inspired me to call the FDA. Here I was in a phone booth, outside the Smithsonian Institute with a million tourists walking by and a fire-engine screaming down the road, and I am inspired to contact a federal agency with which I had no contacts. Sr. Faustina must have been laughing at this scene as I did just that. Little did I know that the Holy Spirit would lead me to Dr. Chen, medical team leader of the Cardio-Renal Division of the FDA. He then referred me to Dr. Packer, a cardiologist at Columbia Presbyterian Hospital in New York City and one of the country's experts in congestive heart failure.

Throughout the process our family kept seeing the word "fish." Now I felt God inspiring me to "reel in the big fish." I was not certain what this meant but I earnestly began to prepare a medical packet for Dr Packer to review, working all of my spare time, day and night, to do so, even though I had no deadline. The stress during this phase of the process was overwhelming. With tears of frustration, I felt I could not proceed further. It was time now for my oldest sister, Ann Marie, to play her critical role. She saw me crying and, feeling inspired, immediately stepped in to help me complete the packet. We finished at 1:00 a. m. the next morning. Upon receiving the packet, Dr. Packer, although supportive and sympathetic to my inquiry, felt that another one of his colleagues, Dr. Valentin Fuster, would be a better advocate and referred me to him.

I initially attempted to contact Dr. Fuster through his social worker, Martha Salazar. When we first spoke over the telephone, she stated, prophetically, "You have hooked the Big Fish." It turned out that Dr. Fuster was arguably the world's most renowned heart surgeon. There was simply nobody better qualified as an advocate before the Vatican tribunal. In addition to being Director of the Cardiovascular Institute at Mount Sinai Hospital in New York City, he was also the world's only Triple Crown Cardiologist. As if his credentials were not impressive enough, he had just been named President of the American Heart Association that very same week.

Through Martha, who responded to the Holy Spirit's grace by being receptive to my need to communicate with Dr. Fuster, I was able to proceed with the final phase of our mission to substantiate Fr. Ron's healing as a miracle through the intercession of Sr. Faustina. Martha was always "on track" with me. She was my sole contact for reaching such an important and prestigious person as Dr. Fuster. Without her help, our mission would not have succeeded. Our train was heading in the right direction and we could see the light at the end of the tunnel. However, our mission was far from over.

Dr. Fuester and his wife Maria with Father Pytel in Rome
the evening before Sister Faustina's canonization

Once again, God called our family to do His work. Working closely with Fr. Pytel, his good friend and seminary classmate Fr. Larry Gesy, and Fr. Michalenko, we delved through stacks and stacks of medical records. My son Harry assisted me by working long hours on the computer making graphs of information so Dr. Fuster could easily evaluate it. When we were finished, we had compiled five books of summarized medical evidence for Dr. Fuster to review. The "Faustina Team" would become the forensic scientists of the cause, looking at, and evaluating, every piece of medical evidence.

At this critical point in the process my mother had unwavering faith that Blessed Faustina would become a saint. Undaunted in her convictions, she encouraged everyone, including Fr. Michelenko and Fr. Pytel, to press on. I remember her on one occasion pretending to march at Sr. Faustina's canonization, two years before the Swiss guards actually did so. She told us we were 99% done. I could not imagine what the remaining 1% was, but it would be revealed in early 1999 when Fr. Michalenko wanted to mail Dr. Fuster's conclusion to Rome. My mother was totally emphatic that Fr. Michalenko had to deliver it in person. Reluctantly, he followed her advice. Without this personal delivery, Dr. Fuster's involvement in the case probably would not have been accepted as an official document to substantiate Fr. Pytel's healing as a miracle. As it turned out, Fr. Michalenko had to personally walk this critical piece of evidence through the Vatican to get it accepted by the tribunal.

Several months later Dr. Fuster was called to Rome to meet with the Vatican Board of Italian doctors from the Congregation for the Causes of Saints. Fr. Pytel also went to Rome. However, my mother felt inspired that Fr. Larry Gesy also had to go and urged him to do so. He, like Fr. Michalenko, recognized her insight and did so. As it turned out, Fr Gesy's testimony proved critical, as he was able to speak in depth with Dr. Fuster about Fr. Pytel's condition before, during, and after his surgery and subsequent healing.

Sr. Patricia, of the Church of Sancto Spirito in Rome, thanks Marta Kulhan for her contribution to the canonization cause of Sister Faustina

As everything started coming together, we had to overcome one last challenge. In order for Dr Fuster's summation and conclusion to reach Rome prior to the Tribunal's meeting, we had to hand-deliver it to Fr. Pytel and Fr. Gesy at Newark Airport before they left. We could not send it with Dr. Fuster when he left the next day as it would arrive too late. Martha had the letter and was on her way to deliver it when she was robbed. Ironically, they took her purse but she saved the envelope with this key piece of evidence by carrying it separately. Traumatized, we rushed to take it from her and hand it over to the priests as they left. Despite a traffic jam, we managed to make it to Newark Airport and caught Fr. Pytel and Fr. Gesy on the stairwell in the airline terminal as they were about to board their flight. We accomplished all of this through the grace of God on the 11th hour on November 14, 1999 at 3:00 p.m. (Divine Mercy Hour).

The Vatican tribunal met on November 16, 1999 to cast the final vote to accept or reject Fr. Pytel's healing as a miracle performed at the intercession of Sr. Faustina. Each of the five voting doctors received a special bound red book that summarized Fr. Pytel's medical case. These books, titled: "Congregation causes Sanctorum P. N. 1123 – the CRACOVIEN – POSITO SUPER MIRACULO – CANONIZATION BEATA MARIE FAUSTINAE" are now a permanent part of the Vatican archives. They contain the medical evidence compiled by the Kulhan family and Dr. Fuster's analysis and conclusions.

On November 16, 1999, at 9:15 a.m., Dr. Fuster entered the room where the tribunal was meeting to defend the case to the voting doctors. My mother, Sonia, and I all woke up at the exact same time in the United States, at 3:15 a.m. Deciding to join our hearts with Fr. Pytel, Fr. Gesy, and Dr. Fuster, we prayed the Chaplet of Divine Mercy together. After a lengthy discussion, the doctors voted 4 to 5 to declare Fr. Pytel's healing a miracle. We had a new saint in heaven!

When Fr. Pytel called me from Rome to tell me the news, I was so excited I could hardly speak through my tears of joy and gratitude. We sent flowers to Martha, Dr Fuster, Fr. Michalenko, and Fr Pytel's church in Baltimore, MD, with a special card that said: "Thanks for Believing in Miracles."

Finally, on April 30, in the jubilee year of 2000, our family witnessed Blessed Faustina become the first saint of the millennium. As the bells tolled at St. Peter's Square in Rome that day, we watched as crowds of cheering people from all over the world waived their white handkerchiefs in celebration as Pope John Paul II, assisted by Fr. Michalenko, Fr. Pytel, and Fr. Gesy, celebrated mass on this first Feast of Divine Mercy. There we were: my parents, John and Marta, my sisters Ann Marie, Jean, and Sonia, and me and my two children Harry and Annette, waiving our own Saint Faustina banner for all to see.

When the celebration began, an indescribable feeling of astonishment overcame us. Looking outward toward the vast sea of people, our eyes filled with tears of joy as we embraced each other. Moments later Sonia and I gazed in awe at the exquisitely embroidered tapestry of Divine Mercy and Saint Faustina, draped elegantly from the balcony in St. Peter's square. Then together, with respect and honor, we all saluted Saint Faustina as she ascended the ladder to heaven as a new saint.

Our conviction in the truth inspired by the Holy Spirit had led us to this glorious occasion. Standing there with love in our hearts we found it hard to fathom how our humble family could have played such an instrumental role in the Divine Mercy mission. Yet on this special day, the Kulhans had helped make history!

The Kulhan family in Rome with Father Seraphim Michalenko on the evening before Sister Faustina's Canonization

Chapter 6, Father Ron Pytel's Personal Testimony

In Loving Memory
Rev. Ronald P. Pytel
1947 - 2003

Photo © *The Catholic Review*, Reprinted with Permission

My name is Father Ronald Pytel, and I am the pastor of Holy Rosary Church in Baltimore, Maryland. Our parish church is the Archdiocesan Shrine for Divine Mercy. It is also noteworthy to mention that Pope John Paul II visited and prayed in Holy Rosary Church in 1976 when he was Karol Cardinal Wojtyla. The Divine Mercy Shrine at Holy Rosary was dedicated on the first feastday of Blessed Faustina.

I have been a priest for 26 years. I was ordained at Holy Rosary Church, which is my home parish. I am of Polish ethnic background. My parents were born in America, but my grandparents came from Poland.

As a young boy, I remember seeing the Image Of Divine Mercy in our school with the inscription "Jezu, ufam Tobie!" It was not until 1987, however, that I first became very well acquainted with the devotion to Divine Mercy and the chaplet while on a pilgrimage to Medjugorje.

In the Archdiocese of Baltimore, Bishop John Ricard started the Divine Mercy devotions and Mercy Sunday at the Cathedral of Mary our Queen in 1991. As the devotion grew, Holy Rosary Church became the second site for Mercy Sunday. The first Mercy Sunday Celebration at Holy Rosary was held on the day of Blessed Faustina's Beatification. On her first feastday, a permanent shrine was blessed at Holy Rosary at the spot where Cardinal Wojtyla prayed. From Blessed Faustina's first feastday until the present, we celebrate Mercy Devotions every Second Sunday of the month at this shrine in English, every third Sunday of the month in Polish and a perpetual novena is celebrated every Thursday at noon. We also have days of recollection, pilgrimages and talks on Divine Mercy. It is interesting to note that last Mercy Sunday, devotions were celebrated in the Archdiocese of Baltimore at 37 different locations.

All of this is to give you some background information and to set the stage for my story. Throughout the winter and spring of 1995, I was suffering from what seemed like a cold and allergies. Eventually, it seemed like I had developed bronchitis. I could not get my breath when going up a flight of stairs, and I was constantly coughing. I made an appointment with a local general medical doctor who confirmed that I was suffering from allergic bronchitis. He also said, however, that my heart murmur, which I knew I had since I was a boy, seemed extremely exaggerated, and he-made an appointment for me to have a Doppler echocardiogram.

The echocardiogram was taken on June 7, 1995. It showed that my aorta was stenotic, that a calcium dome had formed over the valve, and that I was only getting about 20 % blood flow through the valve and some was backwashing. In essence, I was in cardiac heart failure. On June 8th, I had an emergency appointment with Dr. Nicholas Fortuin, an eminent cardiologist from the world-renowned Johns Hopkins Hospital in Baltimore. Dr. Fortuin is considered one of the best cardiologists in the United States. Dr. Fortuin read the echocardiogram and confirmed the stenosis of the aortic valve. He prescribed medication and sent me home for complete bed rest while he arranged for a surgical team to perform surgery at Johns Hopkins Hospital.

On the morning of June 14th, my best priest friend, Father Larry Gesy, took me to Johns Hopkins Hospital at 6:30 A. M. On the way to the hospital, Father Larry said to me, "Don't worry, Ron, this is all about Divine Mercy." I underwent my heart surgery at the beginning of the Novena, before the feast of the Sacred Heart of Jesus. Included in the things which I packed for the hospital stay was the Diary of Blessed Faustina. Even though I did not like the thought of cardiac surgery, I was at peace. I just knew all would be fine.

After the surgery, I was then put in cardiac intensive care until noon the next day. After the respirator and stomach drainage tubes were removed, I was moved into a private room on the cardiac floor. The nurses had me up and walking Thursday afternoon. I was released from the hospital on Monday, June 19th, five days after surgery.

During my recovery, I read the Diary of Blessed Faustina whenever I could. I also prayed the chaplet everyday.

After the surgery had been performed, Dr. Peter Green, the surgeon, met with Father Larry Gesy and told him that prior to the operation, I had suffered serious damage to the left ventricle of my heart. Since the valve was so stenotic, the left ventricle was trying to push blood which was not going through the valve; if the surgery had not been performed, I would not have lived much longer.

Shortly after leaving the hospital, I developed pleurisy on July 7th. Even though I should have been in excruciating pain, I detected something was wrong only because I developed a fever. I had no pain. I was re-admitted to the hospital with a liter of fluid on my left lung. My lung was drained of the fluid. I was given antibiotics and observed as blood cultures were taken to make sure that there was no infection going to the heart. When the doctors were sure I was out of danger, and my oral medication was regulated, I was discharged from the hospital. My normal weight of about 165 pounds had dropped to 144 pounds. I looked like the victim of a concentration camp.

July 4, 1995
Father Ronald Pytel.

Father Ron Pytel struggles to eat with his heart condition prior to being healed through the miraculous intercession of Sister Faustina

Gradually during July and August, I regained some weight and strength. I visited Dr. Fortuin in August. After the examination, Father Larry Gesy who had accompanied me had his examination. Fr. Larry discussed my situation at length with Dr. Fortuin who said that he did not know what kind of life I would be able to resume. He did not think that I would resume any normal schedule. He also said I was un-insurable. My longevity was certainly shortened, and Dr. Fortuin's prognosis was not optimistic. The damage to the left ventricle was quite serious. The situation had been pushed to the maximum before surgery. I had indeed been in congestive heart failure which was masked by what I thought were allergies and bronchitis. Father Larry was startled and shocked by this information. Fr. Larry gradually shared the prognosis with me.

I returned to the parish in early September. I was, however, on a restricted schedule.

On October 5th, we celebrated an all day vigil before the Blessed Sacrament, with prayers, chaplet of Divine Mercy, Rosary and talks on our Lord's Gift of Mercy. The day concluded with a concelebrated Mass. All of this was in preparation for the Holy Father's visit to Baltimore on October 8th. I was the celebrant of the Mass. I spoke about trust and how I felt the Lord was touching me with his mercy. Physically, I was feeling and looking somewhat better. That evening, a group of individuals who have a ministry entitled "Our Father's Work", prayed over me for continued healing. Blessed Faustina was invoked to join in the prayer, and I venerated a first class relic of Blessed Faustina. During the prayer, I rested in the Holy Spirit. I laid on the floor for about 15 minutes. I was totally conscious and awake, but I could not move. I felt like I was paralyzed as the healing ministry and my parishioners gathered around me and prayed. Later that evening, I realized that I had forgotten to take my heart medication. I took the medication around midnight, and was relaxing before going to bed. I began to have chest discomforts when I took a deep breath.

Up until this time, I had no chest pains except from the incision in the chest after surgery. This was something new. I felt that I probably had been too active that day.

This pain was present every day after that, but it would be stronger at certain times during the day. The following Sunday, when the Holy Father visited Baltimore, our bus was parked 1.6 kilometers from the stadium. After the Mass, two people were missing from the bus. One person was my mother. I ran between the bus and the stadium five or six times looking for the missing people. I experienced no trouble breathing, and it was a very warm October day.

The pain persisted every day, and I decided to take some time to retreat at the ocean. While I was there, I realized that the pain was the strongest after I took the heart medication. The next day, I did not take the medication, and there was no pain.

I called Dr. Fortuin and told him of the problem. I felt that the heart medication, zestril, which he had prescribed for me, caused the problem. Dr. Fortuin told me that this was the best possible medication for my heart condition, and that I had already tolerated the medication for 2 months with no reaction. He told me, however, that if I felt that my body was telling me something, to try alternating between a half dosage and a full dosage to see if that helped and to call him in a week. The half dosage was better. The pain was less severe and dissipated more quickly. I called Dr. Fortuin and told him the results, and he told me to stay on the half dosage until my appointment with him in 9 days.

On November 9th, I once again visited Dr. Fortuin for a scheduled appointment. After an initial examination, a Doppler echocardiogram was taken. Dr. Fortuin viewed the results of the test and then called me into his office. He stared at me in silence for what seemed like an eternity and then he spoke. To the best of my recollection, these were his exact words: "Ron, someone has intervened for you." I asked, "what do you mean?" he said: "Your heart is normal." I said "What?" And he repeated, "your heart is normal." I responded, "Well, Dr. Green, the surgeon had suggested that you do an echocardiogram to see if the left ventricle was strengthening.' And Dr. Fortuin said, "No, no ... we're talking normal. I was not at all optimistic about your condition. I can't explain it." He continued: "you have no restrictions, you are to take no medication except the coumadin, and I'll see you in a year." I responded, "A year?" he said, "Yeah, a year. Your heart is normal."

Dr. Fortuin then reminded me that I needed the blood thinners because of the artificial valve, and to continue to get my blood-clotting factor checked every month so he could check the dosage. He told me to discontinue the fluid pills, potassium and zestril.

Upon leaving the doctor's office, I called Fr. Larry Gesy and told him what Dr. Fortuin had said. Father Larry's response was "Well, I guess we got the miracle we prayed for. " In November of 1996, a formal Tribunal was held in the Archdiocese of Baltimore to acquire sworn depositions from the doctors and other witnesses about the change in my health. On December 8th, Fr. Seraphim Michalenko, vice-postulator for America, arrived in Baltimore. I should note that December 8th, the Feast of the Immaculate Conception, was a favorite feastday for Blessed Faustina because the Blessed Mother had appeared to her on that day. On December 9th, Fr. Seraphim went to the Baltimore Tribunal where the documents were sealed and packaged. Then he, Fr. Larry Gesy and I boarded a plane for Rome. The documents numbered over 800 pages in medical records, and about 500 pages of sworn depositions.

On December 13th, my Archbishop, Cardinal Keeler, who was in Rome for special meetings, joined Fr. Seraphim, Fr. Larry

Gesy, Fr. Antonio Mruk, the postulator for Blessed Faustina and myself to present the documents to Archbishop Nowak of the Sacred Congregation for the Cause of Saints. In August of 1998, we were privileged to have Dr. Valentin Fuster, an internationally renowned cardiologist, from Mt. Sinai Hospital in New York, begin studying the medical data. He was so impressed with the case, that he requested every medical record and x-ray, and he studied these for four months. He then requested to see me in New York. These are a few things he said in his findings: "On examining the records and talking with Father Pytel, as well as with colleagues that were acquainted with him during and after his illness in 1995, I became convinced that there was a sudden change, from symptomotology prior to the Healing Mass to complete relief of symptoms within the following three days."

"It is probable that the sudden symptomatic improvement of Father Ronald Pytel following the Healing Mass on October 5, 1995, cannot be explained by natural medical means. " After studying all of the information and results of the repeated tests of the last four years, the doctors of the Sacred Congregation for the Cause of Saints consulted on November 16, 1999. This date which was chosen because of the availability of all the doctors, happened to also be the feast of Our Lady of Mercy (Ostrabrama). Blessed Faustina's congregation is the Sisters of Our Lady of Mercy. Dr. Valentin Fuster was admitted as a voting member of the consultation team of doctors. They voted that this sudden change from a severely damaged left ventricle of the heart to a super-normal functioning left ventricle cannot be explained by natural medical science, it was indeed a miracle attributed to the intercession of Blessed Faustina Kowalska.

People say that the best way to get to the boss is through his or her secretary. There are two secretaries to whom I owe a great deal of gratitude. The first is the secretary of Dr. Fortuin. His appointment schedule was very heavy. Yet when his secretary heard how seriously ill I was, she called me and told me he had a cancellation in his appointments, and that I should be at his office in a 1/2 hour. I found out later that she canceled his lunch hour. Because of her, I had one of the best cardiologists in the United States as well as a specially chosen surgical team.

The second secretary to whom I owe a great deal of gratitude is Blessed Faustina, the Secretary of Divine Mercy. I know in my heart that Blessed Faustina put in a word with Jesus, and the love flowing from his heart touched mine and healed me. It's as simple as that.

Joe and Sonia Kenney visit with Father Ron Pytel at the Holy Rosary Parish Rectory in 2001, two years before he would succumb to kidney cancer

Epilogue, Divine Mercy Today

"Meditate on the Prophet Jonah and his Mission"
(Diary of Saint Sister M. Faustina, paragraph 331).

One of fruits of the canonization for the Kulhan family was a feeling my then future wife Sonia had after the ceremony in Rome that her True Love would come into her life shortly thereafter. She also had a premonition since she was a little girl that she would have to wait until the age of 40 for this to occur. Such would be her destiny when we first contacted each other in December of 2000 through a Catholic singles organization, the year Sonia turned 40 and the same year Sister Faustina became the first saint of the Millennium. The next year I proposed to her on her 41st birthday in Medjugorje. It was on this pilgrimage to Medjugorje that I began to realize the power of Divine Mercy and how critical this grace is for our present time.

Before we left, Father Seraphim Michalenko told us to contact his friend, Dragan Kozina, if we wanted to see "The Miraculous Image of Divine Mercy." Father Seraphim stated that this painting got its name after the healing of a paralyzed man in Italy. While he was venerating the image, Jesus reportedly told him: "Stand up and come forward." He did, leaving his wheelchair behind forever. The painting eventually made its way to a small chapel in a cemetery just east of Medjugorje. All we knew about Dragan at the time was that he could get the key to the chapel from the Franciscans, to whom it was entrusted, and show us the image.

Joe and Sonia Kenney in front of the Miraculous Image of Divine Mercy, and standing outside the chapel with Dragan in Medjugorje on May 13, 2001

We soon discovered that there was more to the story about this icon and about Dragan himself. Dragan had been a colonel at the height of the Bosnian Civil War. Even more intriguing, he had been the commander responsible for defending Medjugorje against the Serbian advance. As a veteran myself, we exchanged stories about the miraculous protection soldiers we had known had experienced on the battlefield. He then started to tell us about the power of the Miraculous Image of Divine Mercy and how it had saved Medjugorje.

Dragan's unit had been battered and morale was low after years of fighting the larger, better-equipped Serbian army. Enemy forces were massing just east of the city for what appeared to be a final, major offensive. It was at this time that the Miraculous Image of Divine Mercy arrived from Rome. Upon seeing it, the villagers immediately felt inspired to publicly invoke God's mercy to save their town. Dragan objected, as doing so would expose the population to enemy air strikes. Undaunted, the citizens rallied behind the image, marching through the city in a solemn prayer procession. The Croatian army, inspired by the faith of their fellow villagers, launched a daring counter-offensive the next day.

Success was instant as Croatian forces surprised the much larger Serbian army and routed them from their well-fortified positions. He showed me the battlefield, which was near the chapel housing the Miraculous Image of Divine Mercy. From a military perspective, I was astonished that the attack could have succeeded. The Serbs were on high ground, with a river running in front of them. They also had tanks, artillery, and aircraft. The only explanation was divine intervention, made even more convincing by the fact that never again would Serbian forces threaten Medjugorje. When we traveled to Dubrovnik later that week, I could not help but notice how towns just 10 miles away from Medjugorje were still scared in the aftermath of armed conflict. Numerous houses had bullet holes in them and many had been reduced to rubble. Throughout it all, Medjugorje had remained an "Oasis of Peace."

The Miraculous Image of Divine Mercy eventually made it to a church in the village where the Croatians defeated the Serbs, in honor of its powerful intercession, to be venerated by future generations. Such would be the fruits of this additional, and also previously untold, story of Divine Mercy.

As the message of Divine Mercy to "Trust in Jesus" gave the Kulhan family the strength to triumph over their extreme trials, and as it became the true source of power that saved Medjugorje from what appeared to be certain destruction, so too can it save our great nation at this most critical time in world history. Only through divine intervention will we ultimately prevail against the evil forces that attack us today.

So now, as in the time of Jonah, our leaders must do what the King of Nineveh did and plead for all Americans to "turn from their evil ways... so that we do not perish." (*Jonah 3:8-9*) For as our Lord Jesus said: "A wicked and adulterous nation asks for a miraculous sign! But none will be given it except the sign of the prophet Jonah" (*Matthew 12:39*)

The valley where the Croatian army routed Serbian forces from Medjugorje and the Church of Divine Mercy (large building lower left center)

Joe and Sonia Kenney with three local children outside the Church of Divine Mercy, present-day home of the Miraculous Image of Divine Mercy

Made in the USA